The
Coaches' Little
PLAYBOOK

Thoughts from Great Coaches
About the Greatest Game of All—Life

GEORGE HETZEL JR.

CUMBERLAND HOUSE
NASHVILLE, TENNESSEE

Copyright © 1996, 2002 George Hetzel Jr.
Images © 1996 PhotoDisc, Inc.

Published by
CUMBERLAND HOUSE PUBLISHING, INC.
431 Harding Industrial Drive
Nashville, Tennessee 37211
www.cumberlandhouse.com

Cover design by Gore Studio, Inc., Nashville, Tennessee.

Library of Congress Cataloging-in-Publication Data

The coaches' little playbook / [compiled by] George Hetzel, Jr.
    p. cm.
  ISBN 1-58182-266-9 (pbk. : alk. paper)
  1. Sports—Quotations, maxims, etc. 2. Success—
Quotations, maxims, etc. 3. Coaches (Athletics)—Quotations.
I. Hetzel, George, 1962–
GV706.55.C63 1996
796'.02—dc20   96-35416
                         CIP

ISBN 978-1-68442-350-7 (pbk)

To my mother, Dottie, whose love of life and sports can only be matched by her love for her family.
Your victory over breast cancer will always be the greatest win we ever celebrate in our family.
I love you, Mom.

And to my sister, Honey, who is today also bravely battling breast cancer and setting an example for us all.
I'm looking forward to celebrating your victory too!
I love you.

CONTENTS

ACKNOWLEDGMENTS

A very special thank you to Susan Thomas for her hard work and dedication to this book. Without your help, it never would have been finished. I feel fortunate that our paths have crossed, and I am sure that you will accomplish many wonderful things in life. I'd also like to thank Sheri Malman, off whom I bounced the idea for this book. Thanks for your belief in the idea and in helping to get it into the right hands. And I'd like to thank Ron Pitkin, my publisher and the founder of Cumberland House Publishing. Ron's belief in this book is the foundation of any success it might obtain. And to Ed Curtis, my editor, thanks for fixing all the mistakes that my English teachers couldn't. You have the ingredient every great editor has—grace under fire. And to my father, George Hetzel Sr., the greatest coach I ever had. I love you, Dad.

INTRODUCTION

I have written this book because I believe that athletics fosters within all of us values and attitudes that help us play the greatest game of all: life. Although it contains the wise thoughts of some of the world's greatest coaches, this small volume is not really about sports. It is, instead, about what everyone gains from competition: commitment, teamwork, dedication, loyalty, perseverance, setting goals, drive, and discipline. These qualities help us later in the workplace, in our personal and professional relationships, and with raising our children.

The ancient Greeks, who gave us our Western concept of athletics, had a special word for winning. They called it Nike! This Nike! or sense of victory, is the enormous thrill that rushes through us when we finish first or when we watch someone perform an extraordinary feat, such as run a four-minute mile or connect with a ninety-mile-per-hour fastball and send it into the upper deck.

One of the lessons I've learned from sports—and it took me a long time to grasp it—is that this Nike! or victory, is only loosely connected to any numbers we may see on a scoreboard. In fact, numbers are only a very small part of the game. There is far more to victory than finishing a couple of steps or points ahead of the next guy. Victory is an attitude we bring to winning and losing and, yes, to life itself. This attitude makes us winners instead of losers.

So how did I learn about victory? From playing the game, of course, from throwing all the energy I could muster into competition and then reaching for just a bit more, and—occasionally—from finishing first. But mostly I learned it from my coaches. That's right, those same folks who go to work in sweats instead of business suits, who wear old worn-out baseball caps, who growl at us, bark orders from the sidelines, turn red in the face from frustration, and blow whistles so loud that it makes us jump right out of our skin. Our coaches are the ones who teach us about winning—on and off the field.

The best—and winningest—coaches are successful as both educators and philosophers. They teach and motivate. When we listen to them—and if we know what's good for us, we better—coaches can instill a sense of self, a commitment to a greater whole, and, best of all, a lifelong dedication to excellence.

Now more than ever, I think we all could benefit from the wit, wisdom, and plain old-fashioned common sense that a good coach has to offer. Kids especially need to hear what coaches have to say. That's why I've created this volume of insights from some of the best coaches America—or the world—has ever known. I hope you enjoy reading this book as much as I did writing it. I hope you will find here motivation and encouragement to follow the ideals of sportsmanship and reach for your own personal victories.

1

BELIEVE IN
YOURSELF

◆ ◆ ◆

My father gave me the greatest gift anyone could give another person—he believed in me.

JIM VALVANO, *North Carolina State University basketball*

◆ ◆ ◆

The only discipline that lasts is self-discipline.

BUM PHILLIPS, *Houston Oilers*

◆ ◆ ◆

The only place you can win a football game is on the field. The only place you can lose is in your heart.

DARRELL ROYAL, *University of Texas football*

Besides pride, loyalty, discipline, heart, and mind, confidence is the key to all the locks.

JOE PATERNO, *Penn State University football*

◇ ◇ ◇

We all like to prove people wrong who say we're no good.

STEVE SPURRIER, *University of Florida football and Washington Redskins*

◇ ◇ ◇

I became an optimist when I discovered that I wasn't going to win any more games by being anything else.

EARL WEAVER, *Baltimore Orioles*

I demand just one thing from Clemson players, and that is attitude. I want them to think as positively as the eighty-five-year-old man who married a twenty-five-year-old woman and ordered a five-bedroom house near an elementary school.

CHARLIE PELL, *Clemson University football*

◆ ◆ ◆

Once a year an athlete may be made insufferable by praise. Once a day a truly deserving athlete may fall by the wayside for the want of it.

BUD WILKINSON, *University of Oklahoma football*

Never let hope elude you. That is life's biggest fumble.

BOB ZUPPKE, *University of Illinois football*

◆ ◆ ◆

With my athletes, they have very different levels of ability. But ultimately it is not as important for them to know whether or not they were the best, as long as they know that they did their best.

RICHARD BRYANT, *Charlotte Wheelchair Hornets and Carolina Tarwheels*

◆ ◆ ◆

Losing a game is heartbreaking. Losing your sense of excellence or worth is a tragedy.

JOE PATERNO, *Penn State University football*

Always have a plan, and believe in it. Nothing good happens by accident.

CHUCK KNOX, *Los Angeles Rams*

◇ ◇ ◇

People always think that kids' sports are about fun. The kids have fun playing, but that's not why they play. The real reason they play is to find out about who they are. It's a vehicle for self-discovery.

PAUL CLEMENTS, *YMCA and Little League coach*

We can do everything that men do, except shave.

CHERYL MILLER, *University of Southern California women's basketball*

◇ ◇ ◇

Security comes from earning it, not seeking it.

MARV LEVY, *Buffalo Bills*

◇ ◇ ◇

The better you become, the more people will try to find something wrong with you.

ROBERT LANSDORP, *professional tennis coach*

No matter what you do, life is selling: selling yourself, selling a program, selling this, selling that.

JAMES F. ELLIOT, *Villanova University track*

◇ ◇ ◇

You can motivate players better with kind words than you can with a whip.

BUD WILKINSON, *University of Oklahoma football*

When things are going bad in athletics and in life—do not get too low. And when things are going great, do not get too high. Make adjustments each day of your life to make it happen in a positive manner.

RON POLK, *Mississippi State University baseball*

◆ ◆ ◆

For young children, sports is a means of expression. At the younger ages, children are physical creatures, and they can express themselves through the physicalness of sports. There is usually a definite correlation between what they reveal about themselves as kids in sports and in their adult lives.

PAUL CLEMENTS, *YMCA and Little League coach*

A marathon is like life with its ups and downs, but once you've done it, you feel that you can do anything.

ANONYMOUS

◆ ◆ ◆

F loat like a butterfly; sting like a bee.

DREW "BUNDINI" BROWN, *trainer for Muhammad Ali*

ACCEPT
CHALLENGES
ENTHUSIASTICALLY

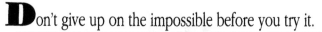on't give up on the impossible before you try it.

BIGGIE MUNN, *Michigan State University football*

◇ ◇ ◇

The athlete who says that something cannot be done should never interrupt the one who is doing it.

JOHN WOODEN, *UCLA basketball*

◇ ◇ ◇

A human being doesn't know how far he can go until he's pushed himself to the limit.

BOB MATTICK, *Toronto Blue Jays*

The difference between the impossible and the possible lies in a person's determination.

TOMMY LASORDA, *Los Angeles Dodgers*

❖ ❖ ❖

Do not let what you cannot do interfere with what you can do.

JOHN WOODEN, *UCLA basketball*

❖ ❖ ❖

How is riding a bull like life? Life is a roller-coaster ride, and you won't get any better practice than riding a bull.

GARY LEFFEW, *bull riding instructor*

Really, it comes down to your philosophy. Do you want to be safe and good, or do you want to take a chance and be great?

JIMMY JOHNSON, *Dallas Cowboys and Miami Dolphins*

◆ ◆ ◆

Ninety-eight percent of success is in the head and the heart.

CATHY FERGUSON, *Olympic swimming*

◆ ◆ ◆

The biggest mistake an athlete can make is to be afraid of making one.

L. RON HUBBARD, *author*

If your work is not fired with enthusiasm, you will be fired with enthusiasm.

JOHN MAZUR, *New England Patriots*

◇ ◇ ◇

Competition is what made America great.

JIM FOSTER, *Vanderbilt University women's basketball*

◇ ◇ ◇

If you're a positive person, you're an automatic motivator. You can get people to do things they don't think they're capable of.

COTTON FITZSIMMONS, *Phoenix Suns*

The only reason I majored in psychology was that my first psych professor was full of energy and enthusiasm. I know now you can't accomplish anything without those things.

JERRY GLANVILLE, *Atlanta Falcons*

◆ ◆ ◆

There are a lot of fellas with all the ability it takes to play in the major leagues, but they never make it. They always get stuck in the minor leagues because they haven't got the guts to make the climb.

COOKIE LAVAGETTO, *Washington Senators*

Coaches should always get their kids to think in terms of wanting to, not having to.

GEORGE RAVELING, *University of Southern California basketball*

◇ ◇ ◇

Extraordinary accomplishments only happen when your passion produces extraordinary effort. If it doesn't consume you, be ready to accept mediocre results.

JOHN RENNIE, *Duke University soccer*

◇ ◇ ◇

You don't get to choose when opportunity is going to knock, so you better be prepared for it when it does.

TED ANDERSON, *University of Nebraska at Omaha soccer*

When you play defense, you have to storm the fort or play cover—you can't do both.

PAUL "BEAR" BRYANT, *University of Alabama football*

◇ ◇ ◇

It was Coach Robinson who taught me that success in sports, and in life, has to do with not accepting failure as an option. More important, he taught me that if you do fail, there's no sense blaming anyone but yourself. And that failing at something once isn't failure . . . it's just part of the process.

BILLY CASPER, *NFL player referring to his high school football coach*

◇ ◇ ◇

Competition makes a horse-race.

OVID *(from* Ars Amatoria, *book 3)*

Competition can damage self-esteem, create anxiety, and lead to cheating and hurt feelings. But so can romantic love.

MARIAH BURTON NELSON, *Stanford University basketball*

◇ ◇ ◇

When you have the attitude of a champion, you see adversity as your training partner.

CONOR GILLEN

◇ ◇ ◇

A racer's greatest fear is not perishing in one of these race cars. It's being injured and having to watch someone else drive his car.

MARK MARTIN, *NASCAR*

Ah, but a man's reach should exceed his grasp, or what's a heaven for?—Robert Browning.

JOE PATERNO, *Penn State University football*

◆ ◆ ◆

Athletics are like everything else. I've never seen a great athlete burn out on their sport, because they truly love what they're doing. People who get burned out on what they're doing are probably doing it for the wrong reasons.

STEVE HAMILTON, *Morehead State University baseball*

In our lives we will encounter many challenges, and tomorrow we face one together. How we accept the challenge and attack the challenge head-on is only about us—no one can touch that. If we win or lose this weekend, it will not make a difference in our lives. But why we play and how we play will make a difference in our lives forever.

BETH ANDERS, *Old Dominion field hockey*

◆ ◆ ◆

Be a dreamer. If you don't know how to dream, you're dead.

JIM VALVANO, *North Carolina State basketball*

The important thing in the Olympic Games is not to win but to take part; the important thing in life is not the triumph but the struggle.

BARON PIERRE DE COUBERTIN, *founder of the modern Olympic movement*

◆ ◆ ◆

Enthusiasm is everything. It must be as taut and vibrating as a guitar string.

PELÉ, *soccer legend*

WORK HARD AND PERSEVERE

The harder I work, the luckier I get.

GEORGE ALLEN, *Los Angeles Rams and Washington Redskins*

◆ ◆ ◆

Good things happen to those who wait, but only what's left behind by those who hustle.

CHUCK NOLL, *Pittsburgh Steelers*

◆ ◆ ◆

A man who wakes up and finds himself a success has not been sleeping.

FRANK LANE, *Kansas City Athletics*

The ability to prepare to win is as important as the will to win.

BOBBY KNIGHT, *Texas Tech University basketball*

◆ ◆ ◆

Sweat plus sacrifice equals success.

CHARLES O. FINLEY, *Oakland Athletics owner*

◆ ◆ ◆

If what you did yesterday still looks big to you, you haven't done much today.

WID MATTHEWS, *Chicago Cubs*

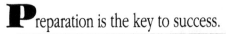

Preparation is the key to success.

STEVE BUTLER, *Miller Place Badminton Club (England)*

◆ ◆ ◆

When I was fifteen, I had lucky underwear. When that failed, I had a lucky hairdo, then a lucky race number, even lucky race days. After fifteen years, I've found the secret to success is simple. It's hard work.

MARGARET GROSS, *track*

◆ ◆ ◆

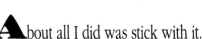

About all I did was stick with it.

PAUL "BEAR" BRYANT, *University of Alabama football*

The most interesting thing about this sport, at least to me, is the activity of preparation—any aspect of preparation for the games. The thrill isn't in the winning, it's in the doing.

CHUCK NOLL, *Pittsburgh Steelers*

◇ ◇ ◇

It is more important to motivate your players for practice than for games.

JACK STALLINGS, *Georgia Southern University baseball*

◇ ◇ ◇

Genius: It's 1 percent inspiration and 99 percent perspiration. No one has ever drowned in sweat.

LOU HOLTZ (AND THOMAS EDISON), *University of South Carolina football*

You can't make a great play until you first do it in practice.

CHUCK NOLL, *Pittsburgh Steelers*

◆ ◆ ◆

Coaches who scrimmage all the time don't know what to practice.

PAUL BROWN, *Cleveland Browns*

◆ ◆ ◆

Never accept mediocrity, and be committed to your beliefs. Live by the Golden Rule, and read biographies to learn how successful people overcame their problems and became winners.

ROY SIMMONS JR., *Syracuse University lacrosse*

The most complete athletes are those who strive to overcome their weaknesses by hard work and persistence. Practicing on one's strengths is more enjoyable and obviously much easier, but working long and hard on one's weaknesses, while it may be the more difficult path to follow, has the certain assurances of success.

AL ROSEN, *Cleveland Indians*

◆ ◆ ◆

You'd think I'd get sick of saying the same things every day, but you can't give up on these kids. Some you pat on the back; some you kick in the butt.

LUKE APPLING, *Atlanta Braves batting coach and Hall of Famer*

I always thought the person who works the hardest, apart from natural talent, of course, wins. I feel the person who works the hardest earns the right to win.

KATY BILDOROUX

◇ ◇ ◇

If you watch the clock, time goes slow. If you work hard, time goes fast.

GENE KEADY, *Purdue University basketball*

◇ ◇ ◇

The quality of your play never counts as much as the quality of your effort.

BUD WILKINSON, *University of Oklahoma football*

There is no substitute for hard work and effort beyond the call of mere duty. That is what strengthens the soul and ennobles one's character.

WALTER CAMP, *Yale University football*

◇ ◇ ◇

1. Stress improvement, not perfection (or winning). 2. Don't take yourself too seriously; laugh at yourself and have fun. 3. Set attainable goals; reach them and then set higher ones. 4. Be positive, walk tall, smile often, don't complain or procrastinate. 5. Prepare purposely, but don't overtrain. 6. Remember—Sports is a game and meant to be enjoyable.

DICK GOULD, *Stanford University tennis*

If at first you don't succeed, you're doing about average.

BARNABY QUINCY

◇ ◇ ◇

Champions keep playing until they get it right.

BILLIE JEAN KING, *tennis*

◇ ◇ ◇

No matter how many errors you make, no matter how many times you strike out, keep hustling.

TONY KUBEK, *New York Yankees*

Offense sells tickets; defense wins games; rebounds win championships.

PAT SUMMITT, *University of Tennessee women's basketball*

◆ ◆ ◆

They say the breaks even up in the long run, and the trick is to be a long-distance runner.

CHUCK KNOX, *Los Angeles Rams*

◆ ◆ ◆

The race does not always go to the swift, but to the ones who keep running.

ANONYMOUS

Paralyze their resistance with your persistence.

WOODY HAYES, *Ohio State University football*

◆ ◆ ◆

One day of practice is like one day of clean living. It doesn't do you any good.

ABE LEMONS, *basketball and football*

◆ ◆ ◆

It ain't over 'til it's over.

YOGI BERRA, *New York Yankees and Mets*

4

MAKE THE BEST OF YOUR NATURAL TALENTS

◆ ◆ ◆

A good coach will make his players see what they can become rather than what they are.

ARA PARSEGHIAN, *University of Notre Dame football*

◇ ◇ ◇

I was a college coach for thirty-three years, and I never believed a boy was too small. If he could play, I'd find a spot for him. You can't have too many good players. Good players win games for you, not big players.

LYNN "PAPPY" SWANN, *University of California football*

What it comes down to is that anybody can win with the best horse. What makes you good is if you can take the second or third best horse and win.

VICKY ARAGON, *horseracing expert*

◇ ◇ ◇

None of us are really born equal. The talented have no more responsibility for their birthright than the underprivileged have for theirs. The measure of each is what he does in a specific situation.

VINCE LOMBARDI, *Green Bay Packers*

Success is peace of mind, which is a direct result of self-satisfaction in knowing you did your best to become the best that you are capable of becoming.

JOHN WOODEN, *UCLA basketball*

◆ ◆ ◆

You can motivate by fear, and you can motivate by reward. But both of those methods are only temporary. The only lasting thing is self-motivation.

HOMER RICE, *Cincinnati Bengals*

I was told by a very smart man a long time ago that talent always beats experience. Because by the time you get the experience, the talent's gone.

PAT CORRALES, *Philadelphia Phillies*

◇ ◇ ◇

My goal is to make the player independent of the coach. The players must be able to assess the problems on their own. Far too many coaches make the athlete dependent on them. This is the insecurity of the coach.

PETER BURWASH, *international tennis coach*

Happiness is found along the way, not at the end of the road. People will soon forget the records. What they remember is the way you hustled, the poise you had, the class you showed.

SHERYL JOHNSON, *Stanford University field hockey*

Ability is what you are capable of doing. Motivation determines what you do. Attitude is how well you do it.

LOU HOLTZ, *University of South Carolina football*

The prospect who does what is required of him is a player; when he does more, he becomes an athlete.

HANK IBA, *Oklahoma A&T basketball*

◇ ◇ ◇

Anyone can be an "ACE": Attitude plus Commitment equals Excellence.

ROBERT INMAN, *Ensworth School, Nashville, Tennessee, football*

◇ ◇ ◇

To be successful, you don't have to do extraordinary things. Just do ordinary things extraordinarily well.

JOHN ROHN

If you want to be successful, you have to do it the way everybody does it and do it a lot better—or you have to do it differently.

STEVE SPURRIER, *University of Florida football and Washington Redskins*

◇ ◇ ◇

It's what you learn after you know it all that counts.

EARL WEAVER, *Baltimore Orioles*

◇ ◇ ◇

Winning ain't no fluke. We got down and got dirtier than they did.

JOHN THOMPSON, *Georgetown University basketball*

The way to run faster is with a four-fifths effort. Just take it nice and easy. Going all out is counterproductive. Our greatest athletes have been the sleepy-looking guys: Joe Louis, Joe DiMaggio, John Unitas. An athlete who wants to die for dear old Rutgers or San Jose State misses the point. He's no good dead.

BUD WINTERS, *San Jose State University track*

◆ ◆ ◆

If experience were that important, we'd never have anyone walking on the moon or going over Niagara Falls in a barrel.

SPARKY ANDERSON, *Cincinnati Reds and Detroit Tigers*

I'd rather have a lot of talent and a little experience than a lot of experience and a little talent.

JOHN WOODEN, *UCLA basketball*

◆ ◆ ◆

I don't care about winning and losing from here on out. If they give maximum effort, that's all I ask.

DENNY CRUM, *University of Louisville basketball*

Leaders are like eagles—they don't flock. You find them one at a time.

KNUTE ROCKNE, *University of Notre Dame football*

◇ ◇ ◇

The measure of who we are is what we do with what we have.

VINCE LOMBARDI, *Green Bay Packers*

◇ ◇ ◇

Just do the best with what you have, and you'll soon be doing it better.

GIL HODGES, *New York Mets*

An artist cannot produce great paintings every day.

BETTY STOVE, *Hana Mandlikova's coach*

◆ ◆ ◆

To improve, you must make your weaknesses your strengths.

PAT SUMMITT, *University of Tennessee women's basketball*

◆ ◆ ◆

It takes no talent to hustle.

HANS SCHMIDT

ALWAYS

BE A WINNER

◆ ◆ ◆

Winners never quit, and quitters never win.

VINCE LOMBARDI, *Green Bay Packers*

◇ ◇ ◇

Winning isn't everything, it's the only thing.

RED SANDERS, *Vanderbilt University football*

◇ ◇ ◇

Winning is only half of it. Having fun winning is the other half.

BUM PHILLIPS, *Houston Oilers*

Winning is a habit. Unfortunately, so is losing.

VINCE LOMBARDI, *Green Bay Packers*

◆ ◆ ◆

Once you start keeping score, winning's the bottom line. It's the American concept. If not, it's like playing your grandmother, and even then you try to win—unless she has a lot of money and you want to get some of it.

AL McGUIRE, *Marquette University basketball*

◆ ◆ ◆

Hard work and winning are contagious.

AL COOPER, *Clarksville-Northeast High School*

They say I teach brutal football, but the only thing brutal about football is losing.

PAUL "BEAR" BRYANT, *University of Alabama football*

Coaching is easy. It's winning that's the hard part.

ELGIN BAYLOR, *New Orleans Jazz*

The more you win, the less you get fired.

ARMAND GUIDOLIN, *Boston Bruins*

Nice guys finish last.

Leo Durocher, *Major League Baseball, Hall of Famer*

◇ ◇ ◇

I never did say that you can't be a nice guy and win. I said that if I was playing third base and my mother rounded third with the winning run, I'd trip her up.

Leo Durocher, *Major League Baseball, Hall of Famer*

◇ ◇ ◇

Training his nine-year-old son, Mark: "How many lanes in the pool, Mark?" "Six." "How many lanes win, Mark?" "One."

Mark Spitz, *swimming*

When a fellow coach told him that Picabo Street would never be a winner because she couldn't follow the rules, he replied: "That's why she will win."

PAUL MAJOR, *downhill skiing*

◆ ◆ ◆

Winning is the thing. If it wasn't, they wouldn't keep score.

WILL ROBINSON, *Illinois State University football*

◆ ◆ ◆

I'd like to be remembered for winning. . . . If it's worth playing, it's worth paying the price to win.

PAUL "BEAR" BRYANT, *University of Alabama football*

If you don't invest very much, then defeat doesn't hurt very much and winning isn't very exciting.

DICK VERMEIL, *Kansas City Chiefs*

◆ ◆ ◆

Winning is like shaving. You do it every day, or you look like a bum.

JACK KEMP, *Buffalo Bills*

◆ ◆ ◆

What you are as a person is far more important than what you are as a basketball player.

JOHN WOODEN, *UCLA basketball*

Discipline builds winners. Winners stay disciplined!

ED McALLISTER

❖ ❖ ❖

Winning is what life is all about.

CHUCK FAIRBANKS, *University of Oklahoma football*

❖ ❖ ❖

When we lose, I can't sleep at night. When we win, I can't sleep at night. But when we win, I wake up feeling better.

JOE TORRE, *New York Yankees*

I don't accept moral victories. I told our guys that in the game of life there is a first place and a second place. And second place is dead.

RICARDO PATTON, *University of Colorado football*

◇ ◇ ◇

You have to perform at a consistently higher level than others. That's the mark of a true professional.

JOE PATERNO, *Penn State University football*

The trouble with sportsmanship is that you have to spend too much time on it when you're losing.

GLEN DOBBS, *University of Tulsa football*

◇ ◇ ◇

There is no virtue like winning and no sin worse than losing.

MURRAY WARMATH, *University of Minnesota football*

◇ ◇ ◇

You play the way you practice.

POP WARNER, *Carlisle (Pa.) Indian School football*

There is no such thing as defeat, except when it comes from within. As long as a person doesn't admit he is defeated, he is not defeated—he's just a little behind and isn't through fighting.

DARRELL ROYAL, *University of Texas football*

◇ ◇ ◇

Winning sometimes sneaks through a door you never knew you left open.

DUFFY DAUGHTERY, *Michigan State University football*

◇ ◇ ◇

It's not so important who starts the game as who finishes it.

JOHN WOODEN, *UCLA basketball*

The only thing worse than finishing second is to be lying in the desert alone with your back broke. Either way, nobody ever finds out about you.

RED SANDERS, *Vanderbilt University football*

◇ ◇ ◇

I think greed is a terrible thing unless you're in on the ground floor.

YOGI BERRA, *New York Yankees and Mets*

◇ ◇ ◇

Self-praise is for losers. Be a winner. Stand for something. Always have class, and be humble.

JOHN MADDEN, *Oakland Raiders*

The only place that *success* is before *work* is in the dictionary.

JOHN WOODEN, *UCLA basketball*

◇ ◇ ◇

If there is such a thing as a good loser, then the game is crooked.

BILLY MARTIN, *New York Yankees*

◇ ◇ ◇

Losers have tons of variety. Champions take pride in just learning to hit the same old boring winners.

VIC BRADEN, *tennis*

There was never a champion who to himself was a good loser. There's a vast difference between a good sport and a good loser.

RED BLAIK, *U.S. Military Academy (Army) football*

◇ ◇ ◇

Winners bring reality up to their vision. Losers bring their vision down to reality.

CHUCK KNOX, *Los Angeles Rams*

◇ ◇ ◇

Show me a good loser, and I'll show you an idiot.

LEO DUROCHER, *Major League Baseball, Hall of Famer*

Don't be a bad loser—but don't lose.

KNUTE ROCKNE, *University of Notre Dame football*

◆ ◆ ◆

You're never a loser until you quit trying.

PETE POST, *Elam Christian School, Palos Heights, Illinois, Special Olympics*

◆ ◆ ◆

Losing doesn't make you a loser unless you think you're a loser.

MIKE KRZYZEWSKI, *Duke University basketball*

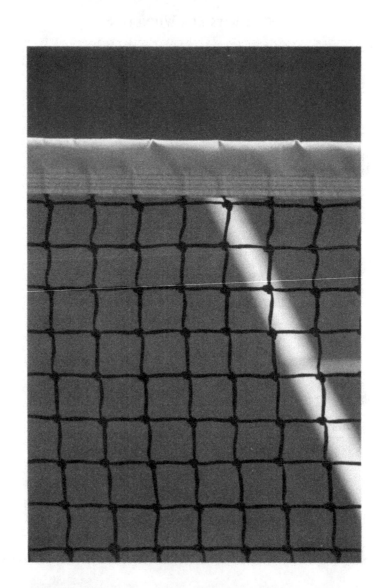

A champion is afraid of losing. Everyone else is afraid of winning.

BILLIE JEAN KING, *tennis*

❖ ❖ ❖

Close only counts with horseshoes and grenades.

FRANK ROBINSON, *Baltimore Orioles*
(also attributed to several others)

❖ ❖ ❖

A tie is like kissing your sister.

PAUL "BEAR"BRYANT, *University of Alabama football*

6

KEEP FOCUSED ON YOUR GOAL

If you don't make a total commitment to whatever you're doing, then you start looking to bail out the first time the boat starts leaking. It's tough enough getting that boat to shore with everybody rowing, let alone when a guy stands up and starts putting his life jacket on.

LOU HOLTZ, *University of South Carolina football*

Never mistake activity for achievement.

JOHN WOODEN, *UCLA basketball*

To achieve in sports you first have to have a dream, and then you must act on that dream. The best athletes are those who truly enjoy what they are doing and display a tremendous work ethic. They continue to persevere in spite of setbacks and never lose sight of their ultimate goal.

DIANNE HOLUM, *U.S. Olympic speed skating*

◇ ◇ ◇

An athlete's greatest glory lies not in never falling, but in rising every time he falls.

NORM VAN BROCKLIN, *Minnesota Vikings and Atlanta Falcons*

Establish realistic goals, and focus on the steps necessary to accomplish them. Practice good training and work habits because hard work, self-discipline, and sportsmanship are the ingredients that make a champion in any sport.

ELVIS R. GREEN, *Murray State University rifle team*

◆ ◆ ◆

We always think of competitions as being about winning. But it really has to do with setting and accomplishing personal goals, even if that goal is just to cross a finish line.

SUSAN STRICKLAND MCDONALD

Our staff coached football in the same spirit as the three Baptists who, upon being shipwrecked on a desert island, immediately set a Sunday school attendance goal of four.

GRANT TEAFF, *Baylor University football*

Statistics are like bikinis—they show a lot, but never everything.

LOU PINIELLA, *Seattle Mariners*

Personal sacrifices are really the beginning of the end of everything because you don't win because you do one thing or two things right. You win because you do one thousand little things right throughout the year.

SUSAN BUTCHER, *Iditarod champion*

◆ ◆ ◆

A person's attitude, effort, and commitment provide the power and passion that make unique and special things happen.

JILL STERKLEL, *University of Texas women's swimming*

Each day your team and each player on the team either gets better or worse—there is no such thing as status quo.

HUGH T. CAMPBELL, *Canadian and NFL football*

◇ ◇ ◇

First master the fundamentals.

LARRY BIRD, *Indiana Pacers*

◇ ◇ ◇

The moment of enlightenment is when a person's dreams of possibilities become images of probabilities.

VIC BRADEN, *tennis*

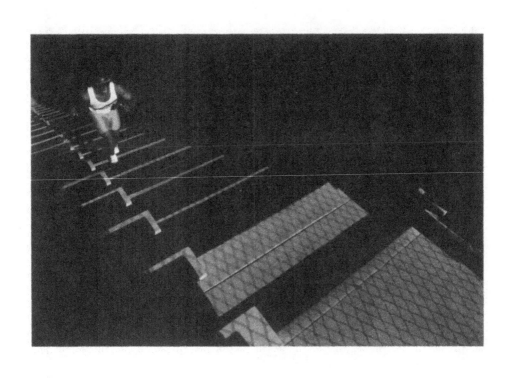

There's nothing so uncertain as a sure thing.

SCOTTY BOWMAN, *Detroit Red Wings*

◇ ◇ ◇

If you care enough for a goal you will almost certainly attain it.

WILLIAM JAMES

I want you to go out and get this one for the Gipper.

KNUTE ROCKNE, *University of Notre Dame football*

◇ ◇ ◇

My horses get the best hay in the country. It is grown specially in Washington State and vanned across the country to my barn. My horses are bedded down in the best straw money can buy. If I have a stakes horse running anywhere but at Belmont, I take him to the track in a private van. . . . Why should I spend months working on a horse, then load him into a van with a lot of other horses and run the risk that he will be kicked?

FRANK "PANCHO" MARTIN, *horse trainer*

You have to just keep looking straight ahead. The scenery may be nice or ugly on either side, but you can't look. All that matters is what's in front of you.

GARY BARNETT, *University of Colorado football*

Never give up.

JIM VALVANO, *North Carolina State University basketball*

7

BE A TEAM
PLAYER

◆ ◆ ◆

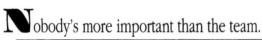obody's more important than the team.

REJEAN HOULE, *Montreal Canadiens*

◆ ◆ ◆

 team that won't be beaten can't be beaten.

BILL ROPER, *Princeton University football*

◆ ◆ ◆

 star can win any game; a team can win every game.

JACK RAMSAY, *National Basketball Association*

On a good team there are no superstars. There are great players who show they are great players by being able to play with others as a team. They have the ability to be superstars, but if they fit into a good team, they make sacrifices, they do the things necessary to help the team win. What the numbers are in salaries or statistics don't matter; how they play together does.

RED HOLZMAN, *New York Knicks*

◇ ◇ ◇

Anytime you really want to know what a kid is all about, place him in authority.

AMOS ALONZO STAGG, *football and basketball*

Deep down, all athletes yearn for discipline.

JOE PATERNO, *Penn State University football*

◆ ◆ ◆

Discipline is not a nasty word.

PAT RILEY, *Los Angeles Lakers, New York Knicks, and Miami Heat*

◆ ◆ ◆

It's important that people know what you stand for—and what you won't stand for.

MARY WALDRIP

We don't want the athlete here who can't stand criticism. We only practice two hours a day, and I can't waste time whispering in people's ears. I tell the players there are only two times when I'm going to stop criticizing them—when they become perfect or when I've given up on them.

—————————————————————————

RALPH MILLER, *Oregon State University basketball*

◆ ◆ ◆

My players can wear their hair as long as they want and dress any way they want. That is, if they can afford to pay their own tuition, meals, and board.

—————————————————————————

EDDIE ROBINSON, *Grambling State University football*

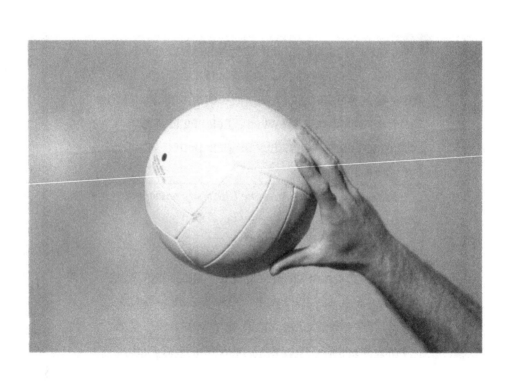

Great football coaches have the vision to see, the faith to believe, the courage to do, and twenty-five great players.

MARV LEVY, *Buffalo Bills*

Champions separate the important from the unimportant. They know that good press, playing time, or individual honors aren't as important as knowing that you and your teammates have responded to the challenge together.

DON SHAW, *Stanford University women's volleyball*

I believe human dignity is vital. You can only succeed when people are communicating, not just from the top down but in complete interchange.

BILL WALSH, *San Francisco Forty-Niners*

◆ ◆ ◆

You can accomplish a lot if you don't worry about who gets the credit.

BILL ARNSPARGER, *Miami Dolphins and San Diego Chargers*

◆ ◆ ◆

When you want to win a game, you have to teach. When you lose a game, you have to learn.

TOM LANDRY, *Dallas Cowboys*

Part of life is getting sucked into something with others. What we try to do with our group is breathe together, share the same space, find something outside of just playing basketball. This spiritual stuff brings an act of community to us.

PHIL JACKSON, *Chicago Bulls and Los Angeles Lakers*

◇ ◇ ◇

I'm not into that business of being relevant to kids. I'm not playing on their team: they're playing on mine. We have certain ways of acting here. My kids are not going to come in here and say, "Hey, baby." It doesn't make you less of a man to have respect for people.

JOHN THOMPSON, *Georgetown University basketball*

The best time to make friends is before you need them.

ARA PARSEGHIAN, *University of Notre Dame football*

◆ ◆ ◆

Set high goals, and be positive so others who share your goals will work together to attain them.

JODY CONRADT, *University of Texas women's basketball*

◆ ◆ ◆

Leadership comes from competence. Leadership is by example, not talk.

BILL WALSH, *San Francisco Forty-Niners*

I've come to the conclusion that the two most important things in life are good friends and a good bullpen.

BOB LEMON, *Major League Baseball*

❖ ❖ ❖

Am I a control freak? No. Do I believe in organization? You bet. In discipline? In being on time and making sure everything at the hotel is ready and right? Definitely. I don't control players. I try to control the environment around the players so they can flourish.

PAT RILEY, *Los Angeles Lakers, New York Knicks, and Miami Heat*

Everyone wants to go to heaven, but no one wants to die.

BUD GRANT, *Minnesota Vikings*

◇ ◇ ◇

You must be willing to do the things that are not fun.

PAT SUMMITT, *University of Tennessee women's basketball*

◇ ◇ ◇

There are three types of baseball players—those who make it happen, those who watch it happen, and those who wonder what happened.

TOMMY LASORDA, *Los Angeles Dodgers*

The athlete who spends all his time learning the tricks of his trade is probably never going to learn the trade itself.

FIELDING "HURRY-UP" YOST, *University of Michigan football*

◆ ◆ ◆

Coaches build teams, parents build players.

CHARLES SMYTH

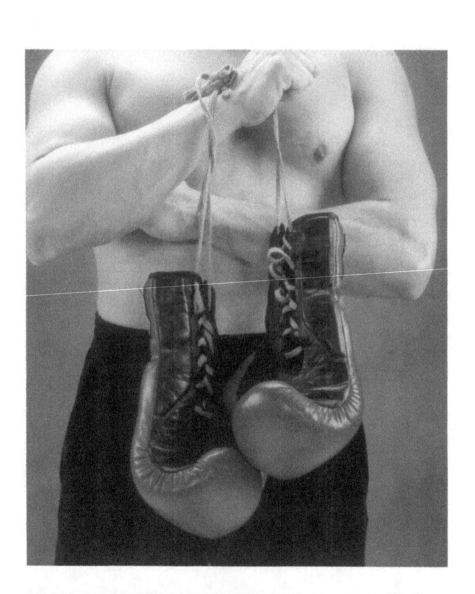

KEEP MENTALLY TOUGH

◆ ◆ ◆

A hero is no braver than anyone else; he's just braver five minutes longer.

RALPH WALDO EMERSON
(He wasn't a coach, but he knew the score.)

◆ ◆ ◆

The first and great commandment is, "Don't let them scare you."

ELMER DAVIS, *boxing trainer*

◆ ◆ ◆

To avoid criticism, say nothing, do nothing, be nothing.

FRED SHERO, *Philadelphia Flyers and New York Rangers*

The battle is not with the opponent, but within yourself. You have to defeat your fear before you step into the ring to be a winner.

GARY LEFFEW, *bull riding instructor*

◆ ◆ ◆

The major joy of most sports is the process, the playing of the sport, and the physical release that it brings. But winning, or at least being as good as you can be, is a major part of sports, and you can experience that aspect only by developing your own toughness, physical and mental.

KATHRYN LANCE, *author*

Everything depends on your mental outlook toward life. If you have a defeatist attitude, it's bad. It's the same with a golf game. It's something you have to work on all the time.

KATHY WHITWORTH, *golf*

◆ ◆ ◆

I don't want to be too philosophical about it, but I do believe some kids need to know you can take a hit right on the nose or the chin, and it's not going to kill you.

BRUCE SNYDER, *Arizona State University football*

The street to obscurity is paved with athletes who performed great feats before friendly crowds. Greatness in major league sports is the ability to win in a stadium filled with people who are pulling for you to lose.

GEORGE ALLEN, *Los Angeles Rams and Washington Redskins*

◆ ◆ ◆

You look at a guy who's being brave. He's afraid, or he wouldn't be brave. If he isn't afraid, he's stupid.

JOE TORRE, *New York Yankees*

Emotion gets in the way of performance.

TOM LANDRY, *Dallas Cowboys*

◇ ◇ ◇

You'll never get ahead of anyone as long as you try to get even with him.

LOU HOLTZ, *University of South Carolina football*

◇ ◇ ◇

To see a man beaten not by a better opponent but by himself is a tragedy.

CUS D'AMATO, *boxing trainer*

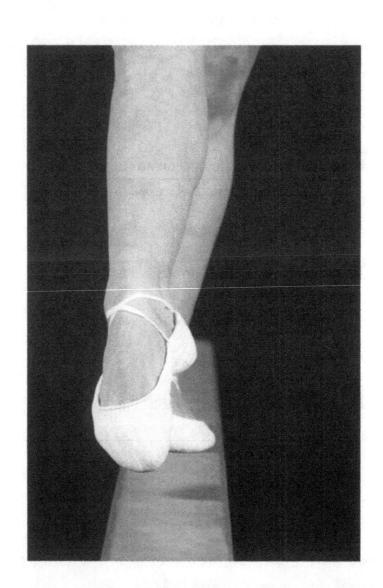

Pressure is everything. We teach the girls that they can't slow down in training for even a day because their roommate or somebody else will eat them up alive in competition. They've got to be careful, or their best friend will beat them. Lie down for a day, and you're finished.

DON PETERS, *Grossfeld's School of Gymnastics*

Publicity is like poison. It doesn't hurt unless you swallow it.

JOE PATERNO, *Penn State University football*

n error is not a mistake until you refuse to correct it.

FRED VON APPEN, *Stanford University football*

◇ ◇ ◇

 fighter has to know fear.

CUS D'AMATO, *boxing trainer*

◇ ◇ ◇

veryone has some fear. A man who has no fear belongs in a mental institution. Or on special teams.

WALT MICHAELS, *New York Jets*

Pressure is something you feel only when you don't know what you're doing.

CHUCK NOLL, *Pittsburgh Steelers*

The point is—and this is necessary to understand the difference between male and female athletes—that in the arena, men take for granted the fact that they are males and concentrate on being athletes. Women never forget that they are females.

DICK LACEY, *New Rochelle High School girls' track team*

If you are prepared, then you will be confident, and you will do the job.

TOM LANDRY, *Dallas Cowboys*

◆ ◆ ◆

I've always envied the kind of coach who could go completely out of his mind and nobody would know the difference.

ADOLPH RUPP, *University of Kentucky basketball*

◆ ◆ ◆

Mental is to physical, as four is to one. It says the truth about the game!!

BOBBY KNIGHT, *Texas Tech University basketball*

I don't believe in a word to the wise—it's the stupid people who need it.

BONE MACKAN, *Green Bay Packers*

◆ ◆ ◆

I think to have long-term success as a coach or any other position of leadership, you have to be obsessed in some way.

PAT RILEY, *Los Angeles Lakers, New York Knicks, and Miami Heat*

◆ ◆ ◆

Temptation rarely comes in working hours. It's in their leisure time that men are made or marred.

FRED SHERO, *Philadelphia Flyers and New York Rangers*

You have to be tough.

MIKE DITKA, *Chicago Bears and New Orleans Saints*

◇ ◇ ◇

Lesson One: Before lousing something up, think!

CHUCK CRANFORD

◇ ◇ ◇

If a coach starts listening to fans, he winds up sitting next to them.

JOHNNY KERR, *Chicago Bulls*

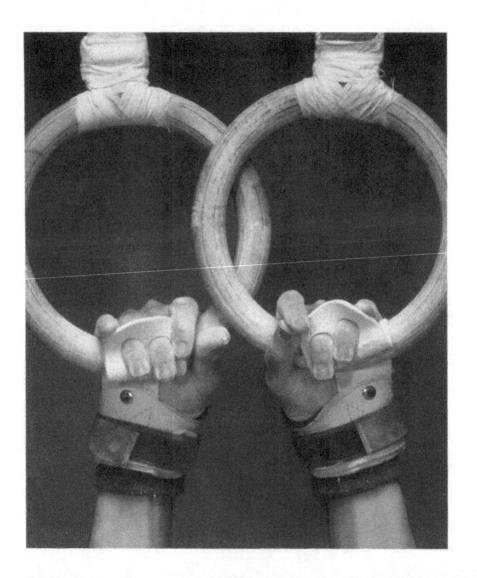

DON'T MAKE
EXCUSES

◆ ◆ ◆

There are a thousand reasons for failure, but not a single excuse.

MIKE REID, *Cincinnati Bengals*

◇ ◇ ◇

Experience is the name we give our mistakes.

FRED SHERO, *Philadelphia Flyers and New York Rangers*

◇ ◇ ◇

The guy who complains about the way the ball bounces is usually the guy who dropped it.

LOU HOLTZ, *University of South Carolina football*

winner never whines.

PAUL BROWN, *Cleveland Browns*

◆ ◆ ◆

Life is 10 percent what happens to you and 90 percent how you respond to it.

LOU HOLTZ, *University of South Carolina football*

◆ ◆ ◆

It doesn't take talent to be on time.

PETER REISER, *California Angels*

You can learn a line from a win. You can learn a book from a defeat.

PAUL BROWN, *Cleveland Browns*

◆ ◆ ◆

When it is all said and done, as a rule, more is said than done.

LOU HOLTZ, *University of South Carolina football*

◆ ◆ ◆

I don't mind playing by the rules. I just want the rules equally applied to everyone.

HARRY WOLBERG, *sporting clays*

When you're a professional, you come back no matter what happened the day before.

BILLY MARTIN, *New York Yankees*

❖ ❖ ❖

You can't go back and make a brand-new start, but you can start now and make a brand-new end.

JACK GARMISE

❖ ❖ ❖

With everyone I work with, I stress the humility factor. Humility should be everyone's final achievement. It is the crown jewel of life. Without it your life will never be full.

PETER BURWASH, *international tennis coach*

An alibi is first cousin to an excuse, and both make lousy relatives.

MURRAY CHASE

◇ ◇ ◇

Anytime you hear a coach say that success is just a matter of luck, you are looking at a loser.

CLIFF SKUDIN

◇ ◇ ◇

There's no use crying over the rules. Our mission is to become successful in spite of them.

STU JACKSON, *Vancouver Grizzlies*

I forgive you this time, but there won't be a second time.

JIMMY JOHNSON, *Dallas Cowboys and Miami Dolphins*

◆ ◆ ◆

You've got to be in a position for luck to happen. Luck doesn't go around looking for a stumblebum.

DARRELL ROYAL, *University of Texas football*

◆ ◆ ◆

Make your own luck, don't depend on it.

DAN GABLE, *University of Iowa wrestling*

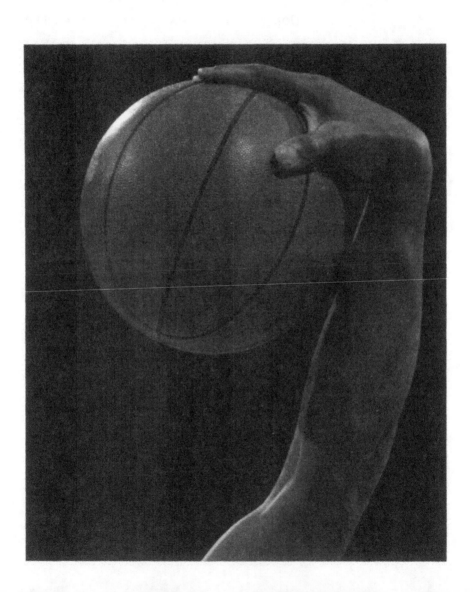

10

SHOW GRACE
UNDER FIRE

What is courage? Courage means being afraid to do something and still going ahead and doing it. If a man has character, the right kind of energy—mental ability—he will learn that fear is something to overcome and not to run away from.

KNUTE ROCKNE, *University of Notre Dame football*

◆ ◆ ◆

The best kind of basketball coach is like a tea bag. It's only when he gets into hot water do you realize how strong he is.

TOM DAVIS, *University of Iowa basketball*

Success is the best builder of character.

ADOLPH RUPP, *University of Kentucky basketball*

❖ ❖ ❖

The true artistry of coaching lies in the individual's ability to do the right thing at the right time in the right place under heavy pressure.

PAUL BROWN, *Cleveland Browns*

❖ ❖ ❖

If you are criticized, then you are important.

DOYT L. PERRY, *Bowling Green State University football*

(1) Be humble in the game, or it is certain to humble you. (2) Your misery is optional. (3) Life can only be understood backward; but one must live it forward.

MIKE SERTICH, *Minnesota at Duluth, ice hockey*

◇ ◇ ◇

When victory is achieved, that feeling can be overwhelming. Keep your common sense about you, and be gracious. Silence is often the best tactic after a win. If you must talk, praise your opponent, and praise your teammates. Never praise yourself.

JOHN MADDEN, *Oakland Raiders*

People don't care how much you know until they know how much you care.

LARRY RAY, *University of Florida softball*

◆ ◆ ◆

My responsibility is leadership, and the minute I get negative, that's going to have an influence on the team.

DON SHULA, *Miami Dolphins*

◆ ◆ ◆

If you don't get bitter, you've got a chance to get better.

CURLEY HALLMAN, *Louisiana State University football*

Win with class, lose with class, and always respect your opponent.

YVES AURIOL, *University of Notre Dame fencing*

Adversity will happen. How a person reacts to adversity is critical. Successful people have a tendency to see adversity as an opportunity to learn something new, to improve, to become a better person, to come closer to God.

TOM OSBORNE, *University of Nebraska football*

If you want to see the sun shine, you have to weather the storm.

FRANK LANE, *Kansas City Athletics*

◇ ◇ ◇

The only pressure you've got is good pressure—the type that makes you run faster, jump higher, and defend better.

RICK PITINO, *University of Louisville basketball*

◇ ◇ ◇

On any given night, anyone can be anyone.

JACK BUTCHER, *Indiana High School Hall of Fame coach*

If you're going to lose, lose like champions.

RED AUERBACH, *Boston Celtics*

◇ ◇ ◇

Class is when they run you out of town, and it looks like you are leading the parade.

BILL BATTLE, *University of Tennessee football*

◇ ◇ ◇

Never say die.

WAYNE FONTES, *Detroit Lions*

11

KEEP IT ALL IN PERSPECTIVE

◆ ◆ ◆

Play sports with a passion, but always maintain balance in your life.

SHARRON BACKUS, *UCLA softball*

◆ ◆ ◆

I have two college degrees, four honorary doctorate degrees, and am in three Halls of Fame, and the only thing I know how to do is teach tall people how to put a ball in a hole.

RED AUERBACH, *Boston Celtics*

◆ ◆ ◆

It isn't necessary to say that a football team loses. I prefer the language of the Olympics, in which you say somebody won second.

TOMMY PROTHRO, *UCLA football*

Our biggest challenge as coaches is not to compromise our integrity, values, and beliefs in our pursuit of winning championships. It is vital that we keep perspective and remember what our role as coaches truly is.

CEAL BARRY, *University of Colorado women's basketball*

◇ ◇ ◇

Great or small opportunities are always going to be there. It's a matter of what you do with them. Take the opportunity today. Enjoy yourself. But whatever you do, make sure you can walk off the field with your head held high.

CURLEY HALLMAN, *Louisiana State University football*

Along with everything else, you need to have fun.

MIKE KRZYZEWSKI, *Duke University basketball*

◆ ◆ ◆

The fans are behind you, win or tie.

STEVE SHUTT, *Montreal Canadiens*

◆ ◆ ◆

Winning is overemphasized. The only time it is *really* important is in surgery and war.

AL McGUIRE, *Marquette University basketball*

Professional coaches measure success in rings. College coaches measure success in championships. High school coaches measure success in titles. Youth coaches measure success in smiles.

PAUL MCALLISTER, *youth coach*

◆ ◆ ◆

Just remember, guys, it's a jungle out there.

THE COACH OF THE KENYA NATIONAL RUNNING TEAM

◆ ◆ ◆

To his son, the NFL quarterback: "The game of life is more important than any game."

DAN MARINO SR.

There was a time when people here did not play sports. It was during the time of protests and uprisings. Our children were preoccupied. The people were preoccupied. Now on Sundays, you walk along and see people playing soccer and cricket and basketball. I think sport is a uniting factor for us—a way to reach out to people of other colors. It can be done through sports. People who play together can learn together.

THULARE BOPAPE, *Thulare Isaacson Primary School, Soweto, South Africa*

◆ ◆ ◆

People who brag about telling it like it is would do the world a favor by telling it like it should be.

RED SMITH, *sportswriter*

On what kind of father he wants to be: "I wanted my daughters to know they could always come to Daddy and—no matter how old they were—could always sit on my lap and hug me and talk to me. They'd always be Daddy's little girl."

ROD CAREW, *California Angels*

◇ ◇ ◇

Dwell on the past, and you'll lose an eye. Forget the past, and you'll lose both eyes.

GEORGE WELSH

You cannot have a perfect day without doing something for someone who will never be able to repay you.

SAM RUTIGLIANO, *NFL and college football*

◆ ◆ ◆

If you think small things don't matter, think of the last game you lost by one point.

ANONYMOUS

◆ ◆ ◆

One of the greatest thrills in life is working with young people, watching them improve, and knowing that you played a significant part in their growth and development.

SHERYL JOHNSON, *Stanford University field hockey*

Abuse leads to restriction. If one abuses the freedoms given to you by people or a situation, eventually rules and laws will be passed to restrict your actions. This is true in all areas of your life, including your government.

LOU HOLTZ, *University of South Carolina football*

◆ ◆ ◆

The toughest job that our coaches have to face is coaching their kids to act like professionals when there are no role models around to point the way.

ZANDER PEPE

When I was a kid, I always dreamed of being a Michael Jordan–type hero. Now I dream more about being a coach and a role model. I like the idea of being a positive example for people.

KEVIN ORR, *Lakeshore Demolition (wheelchair racing)*

◆ ◆ ◆

I found mistrust. I found evil. But then I found basketball, and all the fear and evil didn't matter because I was going past them to play basketball.

JOHN CHANEY, *Temple University basketball*

If the world were perfect, it wouldn't be.

YOGI BERRA, *New York Yankees and Mets*

◆ ◆ ◆

They say that the breaks even up in the long run. But who has the endurance or the contract to last that long?

BUM PHILLIPS, *Houston Oilers*

◆ ◆ ◆

It takes education to be successful in the game of life.

BOB LANIER

A decade after the average athlete graduates, everyone will have forgotten when and where he played. But every time he speaks, everyone will know whether he was educated.

REV. THEODORE HESBURGH, *University of Notre Dame*

◇ ◇ ◇

Any athlete who lets his sport come between himself and his education is the kind of kid who wouldn't study anyway.

HOWARD JONES, *University of Southern California football*

◇ ◇ ◇

I personally believe that every college coach should teach, and should teach solid subjects.

JOSÉ ELGORRIAGA, *Fresno State University soccer*

When you no longer have basketball, be sure you do have a degree.

JOHN THOMPSON, *Georgetown University basketball*

Someday . . . the sun's going to come out again.

JOHN MAYES, *Prairie View Panthers football*

Smart coaches always remember that humility is one play away.

BUD WILKINSON, *University of Oklahoma football*

Winning coaches always remember that there's only a one-foot difference between a halo and a noose.

BOBBY BOWDEN, *Florida State University football*

◇ ◇ ◇

Athletes who make every game a matter of life or death are going to find themselves dead a lot.

DEAN SMITH, *University of North Carolina basketball*

◇ ◇ ◇

Everybody says a tie is like kissing your sister. I guess it's better than kissing your brother.

LOU HOLTZ, *University of South Carolina football*

I have always felt that sports do not build character. They expose it. Hence we are seeing so many athletes today show their true colors. It is a clear picture of how material success (i.e., finances) exposes the deficiencies of character of many of today's athletes. Coaches today have an even bigger responsibility than ever before not to tolerate the immature actions of the athletes. I totally disagree with Charles Barkley's statement that athletes are not role models.

PETER BURWASH, *international tennis coach*

It's discouraging to make a mistake, but it's humiliating when you find out you're so unimportant that nobody noticed it.

CHUCK DALY, *Detroit Pistons, U.S. Olympic basketball*

◆ ◆ ◆

Success is never final, failure is never fatal. It's courage that counts.

JOHN WOODEN, *UCLA basketball*

◆ ◆ ◆

After a 7-3 season, the fans will always talk about the games you won. After a 9-1 season, they will always talk about the game you lost.

DOUG DICKEY, *University of Tennessee football*

When you don't look like you're going to make it, nobody tries to help. When it looks like you're going to be a big leaguer, everybody has advice, hoping for some credit.

JOHNNY SAIN, *pitching coach*

◇ ◇ ◇

I've found that prayers work best when you have big players.

KNUTE ROCKNE, *University of Notre Dame football*

◇ ◇ ◇

You don't save a pitcher for tomorrow. Tomorrow it may rain.

LEO DUROCHER, *Major League Baseball*

A committee is usually a group of the uninformed, appointed by the unwilling, to accomplish the unnecessary.

SYD THRIFT, *Chicago Cubs*

If you step on people in this life, you're going to come back as a cockroach.

WILLIE DAVIS, *Mexican League manager*

◇ ◇ ◇

The first thing I learned upon becoming a head coach after fifteen years as an assistant was the enormous difference between making a suggestion and making a decision.

RICK MAJERUS, *University of Utah basketball*

It's a lot tougher to be a football coach than a president. You've got four years as president, and they guard you. A coach doesn't have anyone to protect him when things go wrong.

HARRY S TRUMAN, *U.S. president*

◆ ◆ ◆

Success should not be measured by the outcome of the game . . . but by preparation, attitude, and effort.

MORRIS JENKINS

◆ ◆ ◆

I will demand a commitment to excellence and to victory, and that is what life is all about.

VINCE LOMBARDI, *Green Bay Packers*

The New York Marathon: a fantastic event.

POPE JOHN PAUL II

◇ ◇ ◇

In life and horseracing what you have to do is expect the worst and hope for the best.

CHARLIE WHITTINGHAM, *horse trainer*

◇ ◇ ◇

The will to excel and the will to win, they endure. They are more important than any events that occasion them.

VINCE LOMBARDI, *Green Bay Packers*

You can make a player prove he's tough so many times that he'll finally stop enjoying the game.

BUD WILKINSON, *University of Oklahoma football*

◆ ◆ ◆

Cast your bread upon the water, and it comes back to you.

GEORGE HETZEL SR.

◆ ◆ ◆

Success without honor is an unseasoned dish; it will satisfy your hunger, but it won't taste good.

JOE PATERNO, *Penn State University football*

Any philosophy that can be put in a nutshell belongs there.

BRANCH RICKEY, *Major League Baseball*

◆ ◆ ◆

When asked if discipline was the most important component of a successful team: "If it was, Army and Navy would be playing for the national championship every year."

BOBBY BOWDEN, *Florida State University football*

12

NEVER LOSE YOUR SENSE OF HUMOR

◆ ◆ ◆

Baseball is 90 percent mental, and the other half is physical.

YOGI BERRA, *New York Yankees and Mets*

◆ ◆ ◆

Reflecting on his Little Leaguer son: "He struck out three times and lost the game when a ball went through his legs. Parents swore at us and threw things at the car as we left the parking lot. Gosh, I was proud. A chip off the old block."

BOB UECKER, *sports announcer and baseball legend*

◆ ◆ ◆

I told him, "Son I can't understand it with you. Is it ignorance or apathy?" He said, "Coach, I don't know, and I don't care."

FRANK LAYDEN, *Utah Jazz*

The secret of managing is to keep the guys who hate you away from the guys who are undecided.

CASEY STENGEL, *New York Yankees*

Spoken while offering advice to young rodeo competitors: "All it takes to be a cowboy is to be a little bit smarter than a cow."

JIM SHOULDERS, *rodeo legend*

To his son, Dale Berra, as he tried to instill character in him: "Don't charge anything to behave; be good for nothing."

YOGI BERRA, *New York Yankees and Mets*

I'm the only man whose wife approves of him going around with fast women.

ED TEMPLE, *Tennessee State University women's track*

◇ ◇ ◇

If you can't imitate him, don't copy him.

YOGI BERRA, *New York Yankees and Mets*

◇ ◇ ◇

Just once I'd like to see the win-loss records of doctors right out front where people could see them: Saved 2, lost 12, tied 4.

ABE LEMONS, *basketball and football*

On why he prefers coaching college to the NBA: "It gives you a nice warm feeling to know you're the highest-paid guy in the huddle."

RICK PITINO, *University of Louisville basketball*

◇ ◇ ◇

When asked by a fellow sprinter what he could do to improve his time, he replied, "Run faster."

SAM BELL, *track*

◇ ◇ ◇

Visiting his coach Vince Lombardi who had just been put in a neck brace after a fall: "Hi, Coach. Isn't it wonderful that 'pain is only in the mind'?"

JERRY KRAMER, *Green Bay Packers*

Don't drink when you drive. Don't even putt.

DEAN MARTIN, *coaching Bing Crosby*

◇ ◇ ◇

[Coaching basketball] is kind of like wrestling a gorilla, you don't quit when you're tired, you quit when the gorilla is tired.

MIKE McDOWELL

◇ ◇ ◇

I don't envy the kind of money that the pro coaches are making. I'm getting paid just as much—even if it's spread over a 125-year period.

DENNY CRUM, *University of Louisville basketball*

On whether he could fill Bear Bryant's shoes at Alabama: "No way. I wouldn't dare walk on water until I learned how to swim."

GENE STALLINGS, *University of Alabama football*

◇ ◇ ◇

On why nobody ever saw him walk on water: "Because I used to do it before anyone got up in the morning."

PAUL "BEAR" BRYANT, *University of Alabama football*

◇ ◇ ◇

No one goes there anymore—it's too crowded.

YOGI BERRA, *New York Yankees and Mets*

When I went duck hunting with Bear Bryant, he shot at one, but it kept flying. "John," he said, "there flies a dead duck." Now that's confidence.

JOHN MCKAY, *University of Southern California football and Tampa Bay Buccaneers*

◇ ◇ ◇

Ability: the art of getting credit for all the home runs somebody else hits.

CASEY STENGEL, *New York Yankees*

◇ ◇ ◇

I don't care how many pennants a manager wins or how much money he has. The size of his funeral is still going to depend on the weather.

CHUCK TANNER, *Major League Baseball*

His instruction to caddies: "Never pick up a lost golf ball while it is still rolling."

JACK NICKLAUS, *golf legend*

◆ ◆ ◆

There are certain things that can't be bought: a mother's love, loyalty, friendship, and a left-handed pitcher who can throw strikes.

CASEY STENGEL, *New York Yankees*

◆ ◆ ◆

We were tipping off our plays. Whenever we broke from the huddle, three backs were laughing, and one was pale as a ghost.

JOHN BREEN, *Houston Oilers*

When you win, you eat better, sleep better, and your beer tastes better. And your wife looks like Gina Lollobrigida.

JOHNNY PESKY, *Boston Red Sox*

◆ ◆ ◆

Pigs get fat, and hogs get slaughtered. So always be a pig.

GEORGE HETZEL SR.

◆ ◆ ◆

When you go into a restaurant and the waitresses' ankles are dirty, you know the chili's good.

AL McGUIRE, *Marquette University basketball*

While on the sideline and "miked" by ESPN, Bill Parcells yelled, "Johnson, get in there—Johnson, get in there" louder each time. An assistant said, "Coach . . . Johnson's in there." An embarrassed Parcells quipped, "Okay, okay, calm down, calm down . . . Johnson's in there."

BILL PARCELLS, *NFL coach*

◆ ◆ ◆

You know our whole program's in trouble when the cheerleaders need liposuction more than the offensive linemen.

ANONYMOUS

On when he knew it was all over for his team against the U.S. Olympic Dream Team: "In the airport when I saw the first five USA players get off the plane."

VICTORINO CUNHAM, *Angola Olympic basketball*

◇ ◇ ◇

Reaction when reminded that the last World Series the Cubs had won was in 1908, and the last time they were even in one was 1945: "Hey, any team can have a bad half-century."

TOM TREBELHORN, *Chicago Cubs*

A tough day at the office is even tougher when your OFFICE contains spectator seating.

NIK POSA

◇ ◇ ◇

Without some laughs, the game isn't worth playing.

BIGGIE MUNN, *Michigan State University football*

◇ ◇ ◇

Hey, baby, the hay is in the barn!

BIG JOHN MERRITT, *Tennessee State University football*

When you come to a fork in the road, take it.

YOGI BERRA, *New York Yankees and Mets*

◇ ◇ ◇

Don't look back. Somebody may be gaining on you.

LEROY "SATCHEL" PAGE, *legendary pitcher and pitching coach*

◇ ◇ ◇

My first major interview? The phone rang, and my wife told me it was *Sports Illustrated.* I cut myself shaving and fell down the steps in my rush to get to the phone. I said hello, and a voice on the other end said, "For just 75 cents an issue . . ."

SPEEDY MORRIS, *La Salle University basketball*

George Hetzel Jr., an alum of Vanderbilt University and the University of Pennsylvania, is the president and founder of Hetzel Entertainment. He is also the creator of the international children's animated television show, *Los Piratas*. Active in many sports as a participant and as a fan, he is an avid horseman, hunter, golfer, endurance athlete, and part-time professional ski instructor. He lives in Nashville, Tennessee, with his Drathaar bird dog, Abe.

If you would like to share a particularly helpful lesson about life that you have learned from a coach, or if you wish to share some of your insights about life you have gained as a coach, the author would appreciate your sending a letter describing them to him at P.O. Box 58072, Nashville, TN 37205 or e-mail him at ghetzel@home.com.